Leading with Impact

*This book is dedicated to Simon,
Alfred and Arthur, whose
contagious passion and enthusiasm
for life is my rocket fuel. They make
my world a joyous place to be.*

GEORGIE

*To Philip and Laura, whose
love and support give me the
foundation to reach for the stars.*

KLAUDIA

Leading with Impact

A collection of insights & wisdom
for today's complex world

GEORGIE DICKINS
WITH KLAUDIA GORCZYCA

WOMEN IN
LEADERSHIP

Published in Great Britain in 2024
by Cajetan, Framlingham, Suffolk.
cajetangroup.com
womeninleadershipglobal.com

© Georgie Dickins 2024
georgiedickins.com

The right of Georgie Dickins to be identified as
the Author of the Work has been asserted by her
in accordance with the Copyright, Designs and
Patents Act 1988.

Design: Jon Allan, TwoSheds
www.twoshedsdesign.com

This book is a collection of wisdom that has been shared
by leaders in financial services alongside other well-known
inspirational quotes. Any quotes that are not specifically
attributed are our own lessons which have been inspired
by personal experience and those with whom we engage.

We have made every effort to accurately attribute each
insight and any unintentional mistakes in attribution will
be corrected in future publications. Our desire is, and
has always been, to make the collective wisdom from all
lessons widely accessible to others who are on a similar
development journey.

Who are Women in Leadership Global

Amy Poehler said "*Find a group of people who challenge and inspire you; spend a lot of time with them, and it will change your life.*"

Leadership can feel like a solitary journey, especially as you advance in your career. That's why Women In Leadership Global was founded. We are an introduction-only private membership and global peer network in financial services. Our members are highly accomplished, inspiring leaders from within the industry.

Our dynamic and vibrant community offers our members a space to connect and learn in a unique and inspring way. Nobody is an island - we all need a trusted tribe! We are acutely aware of the value of peer learning and support, and so we come together to inform, educate, challenge and share our wealth and depth of experience and knowledge.

Our members are passionate for knowledge as well as for community. Our mission is purposeful and that is to harness the power of inspiring women to drive systemic change and advance the face of leadership. In doing so we endeavor to unlock the human and economic potential in each of our members and for that to permeate across their organisations.

This is a pivotal time for women in financial services. Together our community is moving mountains and also paving the way for the next generations.

3.
Self-Management
Regulate your own behaviors, emotions, and actions

Leaders set the tone

Emotionally Intelligent Leadership

Creating an inclusive environment

Setting meeting expectations

Managing your meetings

Giving and receiving feedback

Conducting year-end reviews

Leading challenging conversations

There's always one

Dealing with an abrasive leader

Speaking to an audience

Communicating in a crisis

4.
Self-Care
Maintaining your mental, emotional, and physical health

Maximizing your downtime

Learning to unplug

Resilience during the holidays

Surviving business travel

Energy management

Having a do *not* list

Have a trusted circle

Stress management

Returning from parental leave

Forget about having it all

Find beauty in simplicity

Connecting mind, body & spirit

Create good sleep habits

Laughter is the best medicine

Introduction

Members of Women In Leadership Global belong as a core member or member of a cohort-based programme. For both, we run regular masterclasses that speak to topics which are front of mind for leaders in today's complex world, one where complexity and uncertainty has become our new normal.

We have created this book around the word SELF. We truly believe that all good leadership starts with self-leadership and thrives when joined by self-direction, self-management, and self-care on center stage.

In today's complex world the relationship you have with yourself is the most important one you will have and yet often it is the most neglected.

This distillation of wisdom, insights and lessons was captured from our members and as such this is a collective effort from within our community. It is our desire to democratise leadership and make our learnings available to anyone who would benefit from hearing them, as we truly believe a single insight can shift everything.

We hope *Leading with Impact* offers inspiration, advice and a powerful call to action; to cultivate, bolster and prioritise the relationship you have with YOU. With self-knowledge comes the potential for exceptional leadership. It has a huge bearing on how we draw out the best in ourselves and also in others.

This isn't a book that has a beginning, middle and end. You can of course read from the start to finish, or you may want to dive into a specific chapter or equally you may see where the page falls open. Each time you pick up this book, it is our intention that you learn something new, it sparks your interest or provokes your thinking – or maybe all three.

We hope you take as much inspiration from the lessons and insights as we did from collecting them and we hope this book shines a light on your own self-leadership pathway.

Georgie & Klaudia

Women in Leadership Global

*A source of inspiration and a group
of women who bring us pure joy*

ARIANNE ADAMS	LIZ CARTER	LISA FERNIHOUGH
SANTA AGARWAL	LINDSAY CHOCK	MEAGHAN FITZPATRICK
MARIA ALDOUS	SOPHIE CLARK	STEPHANIE FOLEY
RUTH ANDERSON	CHARLEY CLARKE	RALITZA FORTUNOVA
KIM ANTIFAVE	CATHERINE CLAY	DELANEY GARDINER
ALICIA ARIFFIN	OKSANA COLE	MARIHA GIBBS
JULIE ARMSTRONG	MARISOL COLLAZO	ALEJANDRA GLASS
VIVIENNE ARTZ	AISLING CONNAUGHTON	KLAUDIA GORCZYCA
NOAM AVIDOV	TERESA COSTA	CAREN GRAY
BERCEM BAKSI	HANNAH COXON	SARA HALE
ERICA BARRETT	VANESSA DAGER	JACKIE HARR
REBECCA BERREBI	MARLA DANS	EILEEN HERLIHY
ANNIE BLUNDEN	JOANNA DAVIES	ALISON HIGGINS
GRACE BLUNDEN	SUSI DE VERDELON	JENNIE HOLLOWAY
MARILIA BOTHAMLEY	GEORGIE DICKINS	NICHOLA HUNTER
LEAH BOYD	SARAH DOMBROWSKI	HOLLY JAGGS
GIANG BUI	MADLEN DOROSH	TRACEY JORDAL
CAROLINE BUTLER	FABIANA FEDELI	KATE KARIMSON
NATALIE CARRASCO	MARINA FELMAN	ANGIE KARNA

Self-Leadership
Success starts with You

Self-leadership is the art of steering your own life with purpose. It involves taking control of your thoughts, your actions and your decisions. It is fueled by a deep understanding of your personal values, aspirations, and goals. It drives you toward intentional choices that are aligned with those goals. All of this requires a keen sense of self-awareness to harness your strengths, manage your weaknesses, and maintain a positive mindset.

Self-leadership is the internal compass that will guide you toward success and allow you to approach new challenges with excitement — embracing self-leadership will take you on a journey of self-discovery toward a more fulfilling and purposeful existence.

An Ode to Being

Life can be busy, complex and unpredictable. Sometimes it feels like the world is moving faster than ever and we can find ourselves sleepwalking through life. But we are meant to experience life, not simply endure it.

Let this be your invitation to be still and cultivate the most important connection in your life, the relationship you have with yourself, so you can move from a human-doing back to a human-being.

———

Be Humble
Show appreciation to those around you. A smile, compliment or a few words of thanks can leave a lasting footprint in someone's life.

———

Be Yourself
Authenticity is a superpower.

———

Be a Dreamer
Believe in limitless possibilities that will take
you to new heights.

———

Be Kind
The internal voice you have for yourself should be as
kind as the external voice you save for others.

———

Be Intentional
Success is by design, not by chance.

———

Be Courageous
Do things that scare you and life will expand to meet
your level of courage.

———

Be Comfortable
The "unknown unknowns" are part of the journey.

Be Silent
The world is busy. Silence will transform you from a human-doing to a human-being.

Be Aware
Surround yourself with people who energize, uplift, and support you. Distance yourself from people who drain you.

Be Now
Don't ruminate on the past or stress about the future – you may miss the present.

Be Confident
If you want others to believe in you, you need to believe in yourself.

Be Interested
This is how you will build and nurture meaningful relationships.

———

Be Curious
There is something to be learned from every person,
every experience, every event.

———

Be Open
Opportunities exist all around if you are open to
seeing them.

———

Be Attuned
Your intuition is your internal compass.

———

Be Serendipitous
Some call it luck, others call it chance. If you are
in the right place at the right time, embrace it.

———

Be Creative
Give yourself permission to daydream and have
your most inspired thinking.

———

Be Conscious
There is no change today if you make the same
choices as yesterday.

———

Be Healthy
Listen to your body's whispers and take care of
yourself.

———

Be Accepting
Spend time on the things you can control, accept the
things you cannot.

———

Be Patient
Reserve some of the focused attention you give at
work for those you care most about at the end of the
day when you are tired and irritable.

Authentic Leadership

The core of authentic leadership is being true to
yourself and having a strong sense of purpose.
Authenticity opens the door to a greater connection
to self and others.

*Authentic leaders tend to have higher performing
teams. They do what they say and say what they do:
words translated into actions builds trust among
teams. When leaders show genuine sincerity, display
integrity, and model transparency, it creates
trust and psychological safety. People feel safe
to be who they are.*

———

Authenticity is a leadership superpower with many
benefits when it shows up as being genuine.

———

Authentic leaders are open to change without
sacrificing their own core belief system.

———

Prioritization is easier when guided by an inner "North Star".

———

When you are true to yourself, you bring your impact to the world with integrity, humility, warmth and empathy.

———

An authentically human leader shows empathy and vulnerability and encourages others to emulate similar qualities.

———

Clear team expectations and effective performance feedback creates an environment of trust around authentic leaders. You can beat people into submission, or you can motivate them to perform.

———

Life is too short to pretend being someone other than your true authentic self. We only have one life to live and work is an integral part of it.

———

Navigating between authenticity and conformity can feel like walking a tightrope, trying to decide how much to fit in and how much to stand out.

———

Take the long view on your career. Don't hide the skills and experiences that make you truly unique as they may be your competitive advantage.

———

Remember that your approach gives others permission to bring their distinctive selves to the table.

"The big question about how people behave is whether they've got an Inner Scorecard or an Outer Scorecard. It helps if you can be satisfied with an Inner Scorecard."

WARREN BUFFETT

Calm your inner critic

Most high performers experience an inner critic. The unkind inner voice that creates an echo chamber of self-doubt that you're not good enough, not smart enough, not deserving enough. It is difficult to be polished on the outside while narrating criticism and judgement on the inside.

Moments of self-doubt are part of being human. The antidote is self-compassion. It's often the smallest version of yourself that can have the loudest voice. Left unchecked, it can be overwhelming and derail you, but questioning it can provide useful insights and help control your thinking.

———

Observe your thoughts, but don't get lost in them.

———

Replace your inner critic with your inner coach, the one that rallies behind you, lifts you, and encourages you. Make sure the inner critic is a passenger and not the pilot of your thoughts.

———

In the moments when your inner critic is dialed up on full volume, move your thoughts to what you most need to hear: "I'm good enough. I've got this."

———

When you change the questions you ask yourself, it will change your experience. Interrogate your thoughts. How true are they? A single positive thought can be a powerhouse when you believe it.

———

Leverage your tribe. They can help provide perspective and challenge you to see beyond the limitations of your own headspace.

———

Be wary of going into comparison mode. We can find ourselves comparing and contrasting our inner feelings with others' outer projections. Solicit feedback to make sure you see yourself clearly.

"*A thought
is like a bird
flying by.
Let the bird
fly past without
analysing it.*"

RHONDA BYRNE, THE SECRET

———

Self-satisfaction matters more than external validation. No amount of external validation will sustain your feeling of being good enough. Validation is an inside job.

———

Be the hero in your own story and champion your own brilliance and superpowers.

———

Recognize your triggers and learn to pause before amplifying your self-doubts.

———

Nervousness and excitement have similar feelings. Lean into your nervous energy and translate it into palpable enthusiasm.

———

Value your uniqueness. People who hire you expect you to succeed. After all, your success is their success.

What children can teach us

Watch a future surfer at the beach who is learning to master a bottom turn. Or a child who is getting on a bicycle without training wheels for the first time. Maybe a young gymnast trying to stick a landing after a running front tuck catches your eye. You will notice some poignant life lessons by observing a determined child in learning mode.

———

Commitment will pay off. Progress is often inch by inch. Continued practise will move you in the right direction.

———

There will be bruises. The straight path to success is a myth and is never one and done. The setbacks & falls are part of the journey.

———

Ignore the distractions.
You can't always choose your environment;
you can choose your mindset.

———

Don't allow the naysayer to derail you.
Keep focused and don't react.
Smile at the annoying critic who berates
you when you fall.

———

Have fun and enjoy the learning.
The journey will be more enjoyable.

———

Embrace feedback.
Your teachers and mentors will see things
you can't see for yourself.

———

Not every day will be your day. That's ok.

———

Practice is a virtue. Repetition with dedication and focused intent will move you in the right direction.

———

Timing is everything, so don't react too soon. A bigger and better opportunity may be close behind.

———

Make time for sleep. It is part of your professional armory and yet easy to trade for more time doing. Allow your muscles and brain cells to rejuvenate and repair when resting so you can come back stronger.

"You cannot expect to arrive at full competence without making a start and learning along the way"

IAN CHAKRAVORTY

Managing parent guilt

Who among us has not felt that pang of guilt for being late for pick up (again!), serving finger foods for dinner, or rushing through a bedtime story? Today's world is busier than ever and sometimes the youngest voices in our lives can drive the strongest guilt within us.

There is no such thing as being a "perfect parent", so it's important to keep reminding yourself that you are doing a great job in the eyes of the people who own your parental performance review: your children.

The below list contains some valuable reminders, tips, and pointers. Feel free to revisit as often as necessary!

———

Remember that you are a role model to your children on what work ethic, drive, and ambition looks like.

———

Acknowledge there will be trade-offs. No, you cannot be at every event and that is ok.

Practice the quality of your presence. Children won't remember how much time you spent with them, but they will know whether they had your focused attention or not.

When something goes wrong, you will be there. There will be times when you feel like you're constantly trading off time with your children but know you *will* be there when they truly need you.

Don't forget yourself. It's easy to fall into the trap of peddling hard to keep work and family moving but don't forget that your mental and physical well-being are necessary for achieving a successful life balance.

Some of us love the baby years. Others thrive during the toddler years. Some may be at their best during the teenage years. There is a stage for everyone to connect most deeply with their children without feeling guilty.

"There's no way to be a perfect mother and a million ways to be a good one."

JILL CHURCHILL

—

When there are two people parenting,
do not be shy to ask your partner to take on the
some of the load. There is no need to conform
to traditional mum or dad roles. Your child will
not care who does the baking (or buying), as long as
they have a birthday cake!

—

Embrace life hacks, don't be embarrassed by
them. Celebrate a weekly "leftovers buffet" dinner
when you don't have time to cook; decline
social invitations in favor of a family movie night
where you can hang out in your comfy PJs;
partner with other parents to create a carpool
for your child's very active school/sport/social
life. Your children will have fond memories of any
traditions you create — and double points when
they also help make your life easier!

The wisdom of parents

Many children may roll their eyes and think, "What do parents know?" when they receive a dose of adult wisdom!

We may not have acknowledged it at the time, but there are many learnings we have gotten from our own stratospheric parents, some of which may have even become the backbone for today's daily life.

———

Hard work is a minimum.

———

Life *is* a competition.

———

Discipline and perseverance will set you apart.
Never let anybody question your work ethic.

—

Admit your mistakes.
It shows you have integrity, and it's probably
obvious who the culprit is anyway.

—

How you start your morning strongly influences
how you feel through the day.

—

The small things are often the big moments.
Savour them.

—

Make time for friends and the
relationships which matter.

—

Your time is limited.
Your love is unlimited.
Focus on things that matter.

———

Being polite and saying thank
you will go a long way.

———

Be on time for engagements.
It's a sign of good manners.

———

You will grow or simply get through experiences.
You decide.

———

To all the mums and dads out there,
thank you for the life lessons!

Making fear work for you

There are times in life where fear can feel overwhelming, nearly paralyzing. You know the signs: sweaty palms, erratic heart rate, knotted stomach, wobbly knees, feeling physically ill and having an inner dialogue with the unkindest narrative.

For many of us, these debilitating feelings can have a counterproductive result in pulling back, taking yourself out of a situation, trying to hide, or not putting yourself forward for an opportunity. Afterall, who wants to feel uncomfortable and appear inadequate?

It's in those times when you stand up to the challenge that will often lead to the experiences that provide the most valuable learnings and fulfillment.

Following are mechanisms you can put in place to help you deal with fear so it works for you, rather than against you.

———

Our minds are award-winning story writers.
The reality is very few things are as bad as our
imaginations tell us.

———

Fear is an emotion designed to serve and protect us.
It is the emotional response trying to protect us.

———

The feelings associated with accomplishing
things which scare you can be amazing.
It rebases your level of discomfort. Ask anyone who
has achieved significant milestones.

———

Fear can be your foe or a friend.
You get to choose your relationship with fear.

———

Sometimes fear is a sign that you're too in the
weeds and need a broader perspective.

———

Overcoming fear is a choice. The feeling is real, but you can choose how to respond.

———

Fear presents a sliding door moment. What do you do in that moment? Do you give in or push past it?

———

Breathe deeply. Talk calmly to yourself and take a time-out to step back and consider what *is* rather than what *might* be.

———

Interrogate the fear and understand where it is coming from. Where is the historic evidence to support or refute your fear? Is it rational?

———

Reframe the fear. What if the fear is simply your discomfort muscle but the story is that you're on the right path for growth and expanded opportunities?

"I'm not afraid
of storms, for I'm
learning how to
sail my ship."

LOUISA MAY ALCOTT

Letter to Fear
By Liz Gilbert

Dearest Fear:

Creativity and I are about to go on a road trip
together. I understand you'll be joining us, because
you always do. I do acknowledge that you believe
you have an important job to do in my life, and that
your take your job seriously. Apparently, your job
is to induce complete panic whenever I'm about to
do anything interesting – and, may I say, you are
superb at your job. So by all means, keep doing your
job, if you feel you must. But I will also be doing my
job on this road trip, which is to work hard and stay
focused. And Creativity will be doing its job, which is
to remain stimulating and inspiring. There's plenty
of room in this vehicle for all of us, so make yourself
at home, but understand this: Creativity and I are the
only ones who will be making any decisions along the
way. I recognize and respect that you are part of this
family, and I will never exclude you from our activities,
but still – your suggestions will never be followed.
You're allowed to have a seat, and you're allowed to
have a voice, but you are not allowed to have a vote.
You're not allowed to touch the road maps; you're
not allowed to suggest detours; you're not allowed to
fiddle with the temperature. Dude, you're not even
allowed to touch the radio. But above all else,
my dear old familiar friend, you are absolutely
forbidden to drive.

Luck from intentionality

Waiting for luck to strike may not be a winning strategy, but setting yourself up to be lucky could be the winning ticket. The difference between waiting for luck and positioning yourself for luck lies in your intentionality, that inherent state of mindfulness that is directed toward your thoughts and actions.

You've worked hard, are exceptional at what you do and you're ready for the next move. The next part is where "luck" comes in: are you on the radar when the next opportunity becomes available? If you have proactively put yourself in positions to become known and respected for your proven track record, chances are higher that you will be in the right place at the right time.

—

Setting yourself up for luck involves deliberate planning around the vision you have for yourself.

—

Write down your plan.
Envision what you want to wake up doing every day.

—

State what you want to achieve.
Words make worlds.

—

Be open to everything but attached to nothing.

—

Know the role you actually want. Think like a person
who can do anything they set their mind to.

—

Understand the requirements for that role.
Assess whether you have those requirements or
need to fill in some gaps.

—

Have a plan and know your desired outcome.
Your plan doesn't need to be perfect nor set
in concrete, but it will help you discern where you
invest your time.

———

Goal competition is one of the greatest barriers to achieving your goals, as they compete for your time and your energy. Focus on the goals which will yield the highest return.

———

Work out your own steps and create an action plan for what you need to achieve your goals.

———

Take the next step and the next step will reveal itself. It's important to have the end state in mind, but it's likely you won't know all the steps to get there and that's okay.

———

Put yourself in the spot to grab opportunities when they present themselves and make the most of each opportunity when it comes.

"Intentional days create a life on purpose"

ADRIENNE ENNS

Beware of
diminishing language

*A small percentage of our communication is
expressed using words, so it is critically important to
bring awareness and intentionality to the language
we use, both written & spoken. This applies as much
to our interactions with work colleagues as it does
with friends and family.*

*As important as figuring out what you do want to
say is knowing what to avoid saying. Below are a
few 'rules of thumb' to keep handy so your language
works for and not against you.*

1

Avoid using phrases that undermine your power. This
type of language can creep into your narrative and act
against you by diminishing your self-worth.

For example:

"You might not agree with me, but..."
"It's probably a dumb idea, but..."
"Sorry to interrupt, but..."

Each of the above phrases can be deleted. They make you appear to lack confidence and add no value.

2

Avoid using filler words that undermine your executive presence. This type of language can creep in when you are speaking and you fill the silence with words or sounds that act against you by diminishing your perceived expertise.

For example:

Like
Umm
You know

Record yourself or ask for feedback to be aware of the language you are using and the impact it has on how you come across to others.

3

Avoid using words that create an obligation to the task rather than ownership of the action.

For example, the SMOG words:

Should
Must
Ought to
Got to

Rather than saying you "*should* go for the promotion", say you "*choose* to go for the promotion". The context shifts with that subtle change to help create accountability, responsibility and ownership.

"Words have incredible power. They can make people's hearts soar, or they can make people's ears sore."

DR. MARCY GROTHE

Becoming a problem solver

When facing a problem, it is important to remember that nothing is inherently good or bad; it is your thinking that makes it so. Thoughts can either lead you to a solution or will keep you stuck.

If you question whether your thoughts are empowering you or diminishing you, these tips will help you engage with the perceived problem.

—

Nothing is inherently good or bad.
Thinking makes it so.

—

Thoughts can lead to a solution or keep you stuck.

—

Remember: your best thinking has given you
your best achievements to date.

"We often have
far greater belief
in our problems
than we do in our
ability to no longer
have them"

WAYNE DYER

———

The word 'problem' has a negative connotation.
Try shifting your mindset to think of problems as an
illusion. That will provide space for you to go into
problem-solving mode.

———

Feelings of fear, disharmony, and disappointment
are in our minds. We have choice in how to engage
with a situation and what mindset to bring.

———

As Albert Einstein wisely observed, the significant
problems we face cannot be solved with the same level
of thinking that created them.

———

Sometimes an obstacle is really an opportunity
in disguise.

———

When you experience a challenge, think about what
the lesson is and how you can avoid it in the future.

Manage your boundaries

All leadership begins with self-leadership. Knowing your boundaries and being explicit about them is arguably the most important factor for effective self-leadership. But boundaries are only effective and meaningful if you can also enforce them. Pay attention to how much you gain when your boundaries are in place.

When your boundaries become porous, the following guidelines will help you re-fortify them.

———

Before saying yes to something, do a mental check-in. Do you really have the capacity? What is the opportunity cost of saying yes to this?

———

No is a decision, but yes is a responsibility. Be careful when you say yes because it comes with a different magnitude of commitment.

———

A polite no is ok; placing others' priorities above your own is not in your job description.

———

If 'no' feels impossible initially, buy yourself some time and avoid knee-jerk 'yes' reactions, e.g. "I will think about it and come back to you".

———

Instead of FOMO, the *Fear* of Missing out, celebrate JOMO, the *Joy* of Missing Out. Be conscious in your choice-making, because you really do not have to do it all.

———

Saying 'yes' to more stuff doesn't mean you get to the destination any faster.

—

Be clear on your priorities and their importance to
you, your team, and your business.

—

The confidence to stand your ground comes from
the unwillingness to negotiate your priorities and the
negative consequences of placing others' priorities
above your own.

—

Do not let somebody manipulate you or
steal your time.

—

Qualify your boundaries with conditions if necessary
— when they are ok or not ok to cross. There will be
instances where you need to be flexible.

Don't set the precedent that it's ok to trample over your boundaries.

It's professionally acceptable to defend your boundaries and exercise your power to choose, even if it doesn't feel like it.

Reigning in your people pleaser is critical to success and being seen as a successor; this is the part that causes boundary mayhem.

Be transparent and share your rationale, it enables you to have more honest conversations and removes the possibility for false assumptions to get in the way.

Slay the Sunday Scaries

Have you ever been happily enjoying your weekend and then felt overcome by anxiousness as you realize it will be back to the grind tomorrow? The weekend begins to unravel as your thoughts spill into worry about what you will need to face in the morning.

The Sunday Scaries can awaken nerves as you start thinking about the transition back to the weekly work, office, school and home routine. There's no cure, but there are some tips and techniques to help you keep them under control.

Know that you're not alone. These feelings are fairly common and most people have experienced them at one point or another. It's a normal reaction to the adjustment needed between the different roles you play.

Reframe your thinking. Replace your negative thoughts with more optimistic statements, such as "I can do this!" or "This week will be a good one."

Create a Friday afternoon routine. Before you end your week, check your calendar, reschedule conflicts, and plan the steps for things you need to deliver next week. This will free your mind and allow you to enjoy more of your weekend without an overhang of dread.

Create a Sunday night routine. Our bodies and minds love consistency, so whether it's watching your favorite show, making a special meal, or reading an indulgent book, give yourself something to look forward to.

Treat yourself to a Monday morning perk. Enjoy a treat from your favorite coffee shop or schedule a quick catch up with a friendly work colleague to ease back into the week.

——

Get enough sleep. Things feel better when you've had enough rest, so go to bed at a reasonable time and be well-rested so you start the week on the right foot.

——

Turn work off. Weekends are meant for recharging which is not possible if you spend your time away checking emails. Put your phone away and save emails for the workweek.

——

Make time to get your exercise. Movement is nature's antidepressant and exercise will help boost the "feel good" chemicals in your brain.

——

Listen to your gut. Are your feelings about something deeper than Sunday blues? Be honest with yourself so you can figure out whether minor tweaks are needed or you are being triggered by something more substantial that needs to be addressed.

WITH SPECIAL THANKS TO TRACY RUCKER WILSON
FOR HER CONTRIBUTIONS TO THIS GUIDE

"*This is your Sunday evening reminder that you can handle whatever this week throws at you.*"

UNKNOWN

Self-Direction

*Follow your own
unique path*

A self-directed leader is someone who not only
guides a team toward common goals but also
possesses their own strong internal compass.
These leaders take a proactive approach to their
development, display self-awareness, and take
deliberate actions aligned with their values and
goals. They lead by example and are resilient in
the face of challenge.

When you have strong self-direction, you focus on
setting meaningful objectives and creating the plans
to achieve them. Cultivating self-direction requires
a lot of self-awareness, discipline, and a commitment
to continuous learning. At its highest level of
performance, self-direction is what empowers
you to navigate your own path and make informed
decisions that will help shape your destiny.

Setting audacious goals

If you look at any elite athlete, global leader, acclaimed musician or successful artist, a golden thread between them is the power of their goal setting. They have a plan and are intentional and deliberate in its execution.

It is important to remember that goals are a place to come from rather than a place to get to. Agency sits with you. Define your goals and then take responsibility to implement them so your plan becomes a reality. After all, the best way to predict your future is to create it.

To get started, keep these recommendations in mind...

———

Be specific
You cannot get to where you are going without knowing where you are headed.

———

Plan it out
Break your goal planning down into smaller steps.

———

Goals are useful for setting the direction
Systems are great for making progress. If you're a writer,
your goal is to write a book. Your system is the writing
schedule that you follow each week.

———

Think of goals like an iceberg
The goals are the visible part above the water surface. It's
your daily habits and systems (submerged parts), which will
inform how successful you are in achieving your goals.

———

Strive for continuous improvement
You need commitment to get started; you need
consistency to finish.

———

Progress over perfection
Don't miss a valuable opportunity to celebrate the
small wins along the way.

———

Don't confuse movement with progress
Sometimes more work is needed to reach the reward.

Trust the detours
The straight path to success is a myth; the crooked
path is a journey full of learnings.

Be thoughtful in your choices
Prioritize the actions and activities that will move you
in the right direction toward your ultimate goals.

Give thought to your enablers
The people, events, and choices you make which can
influence how you execute your plan.

Make time for reflection
Revise your plan where needed once more
information is available.

Don't give up too soon
Sometimes your goal may be closer than you think.

"If you don't know where you're going, you might not get there."

YOGI BERRA

Mastering better habits

Wish you had more time? Your habits and how you spend your time will drive you forward or hold you back. Maybe it's mindlessly scrolling on social media or ruminating over something you can't control. Perhaps it's accepting an invitation for an event you do not really want to attend or a meeting you don't need to be in. It's easy to get caught up in these WOMBAT activities - things that are a Waste Of Money, Brains, And Time.

There is an opportunity cost to every moment of the day and every day of our life. Time is a precious non-renewable resource and our personal results are a lagging measure of the habits we have.

How do we instill better habits?

———

Self-reflect

Recognize what activities are depleting your energy and are not directionally aligned with your goals.

———

Flex your self-awareness muscle
Consider where better choices may serve you and
what those better choices will give you.

———

Take action
Better habits do not happen by chance.

———

Small steps, big ladders
Create regular small actions that will take you towards
your desired outcome.

———

Show up and be consistent
It is not the first trip to the gym that makes you fit
nor the first language class that makes you fluent.

———

Exercise patience
Instilling new habits takes time, practice, patience and
being purposeful.

——

Don't let an off day become a repeated pattern
You are human and it's ok to have one bad day, but
don't have two.

——

Build in success measures
It will be motivational to track progress.

——

Start small to make it easy
What's something you can sustain with relative ease?
Think of a habit like compounding interest: little by
little, day by day. A grand gesture that only lasts a
week is not the path to success.

"All we have to decide is what to do with the time that is given us."

J. R. R. TOLKIEN

Prioritizing your time

Do you ever find there's not enough time in your day and wonder how others seem to make it all work? It's not because they have more hours in their day; rather, it's how they focus during the time they have.

One secret of how to better use your time is to understand when you are best equipped to function on the tasks at hand. Our mood and energy changes throughout the day, so if you spend time understanding your cycle, you increase the probability of achieving better results.

Sync your schedule with your energy

Each of us has a chronotype - a personal pattern of circadian rhythms that influences our physiology and psychology – known as morning larks or evening owls. Knowing your type will help you discern between times of day you are most productive – and help you protect your productivity peaks. After all, we have up to 6 hours of true cognitive energy each day.

———

Our days consistently go through a predictable cycle of peak, trough and rebound cycles.

Our cognitive abilities don't stay the same throughout the day and it's best to shape your schedule to the task.

———

Peaks:
Good for work that requires less distraction because you are in better spirits and more vigilant.

———

Troughs:
This time is best spent handling administrative tasks as your cognitive powers are at a low point (as is your mood).

———

Recovery:
Insightful tasks can be most productive when you have returned to a better mood, although you may be a little less vigilant.

*"When
everything is
a priority,
nothing is
a priority."*

SIMON FULLERINGER

———

Manage your energy, not only your time.
Time is a finite resource. Energy is a different story!
How can you monitor the energy usage of your tasks
rather than time they take?

Imagine you start your day with 100 energy credits.
You may have a task that takes 30 minutes of your
time AND drains 30 of your 100 energy credits. Not
the most productive use of time! Think of your tasks
as energy credits and invest them strategically.

· How can you spend more time on tasks that take
  less energy credits and have a higher ROI?

· How can you match your tasks to your cognitive
  energy through the day?

· What one ritual could you implement to be more
  strategic with your energy and fuel up before you
  find yourself running on fumes?

Improving your productivity

Maintaining focus is a cornerstone of productivity. It allows you to channel your energy and attention toward specific tasks with minimal distractions resulting in improved efficiency. Goals are achieved more effectively when you are concentrating on one single task at a time, so it is important to develop strategies to avoid multi-tasking, sustain your focus, and improve your overall productivity.

Below are a few recommendations to help you on your road to higher productivity.

Batch your work
Group together similar tasks such as reviewing email or reviewing reports. You are more productive if you don't switch from one mental mode to another.

———

Remove distractions
Turn off pop-up alerts that can derail your focus.
When stray thoughts appear, capture them on a
notepad and continue what you are doing.

———

25-minute sprints
Set a timer and go deep into one task, whether it's
to brainstorm, write, read, or plan. Allow nothing to
interrupt your focus until the alarm goes off.

———

Time blocking
If disproportionate results come from one activity,
then give that one activity disproportionate time.
Think the 80/20 rule.

———

Practice the 'polite no'
Always respond from a place of kindness and be clear
with what you can say yes to doing and what you must
say no to with regrets.

Comparative advantage

Focus on tasks where you have a unique perspective
or skill set that others do not share. Delegate the rest
and let go of perfectionism.

45-minute meetings with 15-minute transitions

Create breathing room in your schedule to capture
insights and transition between meetings.

Build in regular breaks

Schedule regular short breaks into your day to get
outside or move about.

Remember the most important thing

What matters most right now, either because
it has to happen today or because it will have
the biggest impact?

"*It's surprising how much free time and productivity you gain when you lose the busyness in your mind.*"

BRITTANY BURGUNDER

Making your career goals known

Life is not a meritocracy. Simply doing a great job does not mean others will take notice. It's up to you to effectively communicate your career goals and expectations. While there is no 'perfect time' to have these conversations, it does not mean that 'any time' is good. But with some advance preparation you will increase the likelihood of getting noticed.

Plan now and execute later.

**Show up appearing comfortable
and confident every day**
This is your business card; look the part, feel the part, and embrace the part!

Understand how your performance is evaluated
Know the tangible measures being used to calibrate performance; understand which are most important so you can exceed where it will truly set you apart.

Embrace the qualities that make you unique from other top performers
These are the memorable things that become your part of your 'personal trademark'.

Be clear on who makes the decisions
Get direct access to them if possible; you have a better chance of being considered for opportunities when you are on their radar.

"She remembered who she was and the game changed."

LALAH DELIA

Your leaders don't know what they don't know
Take them on the journey with you; be as confident
sharing your ambition as you are sharing your
performance results.

－－－

**Make the value of your invisible results
both visible and known**
These are the things for which people count on you.

－－－

Create buy-in throughout the year
Meet with your leaders and sponsors regularly; give
them everything they need to advocate for you at the
right time.

Asking for your value

When you're ready to engage in a pivotal career discussion, it will be up to you to know your value and proactively ask for the new assignment you want. A little preparation will go a long way toward ensuring your conversation is a productive one.

Be Prepared.

———

Have clarity around the performance dimensions for your role
What are your metrics of success?
What gets people promoted?

———

The biggest decisions about your career are made when you are not in the room
Make sure your key stakeholders think you are ready.

———

Put yourself in their shoes
Your boss is your biggest customer so ensure your
goals and priorities are in synch.

———

**Determine what your role is worth
and the value of your seat**
Engage with a headhunter to provide valuable data
points to substantiate your position. Factor in your
company's salary structure.

———

Be clear and specific about what you want
This is not the time to be vague or ambivalent.

———

Practice the ask
Prepare the words and the delivery; what you
say is as important as how you say it.

Prepare your energetic state
This is the time to own your value; show up as
objective and unemotional as possible.

Anticipate potential questions
and sources of pushback
Don't let difficult questions throw you off your game.

Take the lead and project confidence.

Keep your information analytical, factual, and brief
Embrace the 'power of the pause'. There is power in
allowing for silence.

Listen
It's a process of discovery to understand sources of
difference and identifying potential deal breakers.

———

Be comfortable with pushback
Ask questions because "no" can be a starting
point for a discussion that helps you understand any
potential gaps.

———

**Don't be too hasty when responding
to a different offer**
Consider what may help you close the gap between
your ask and the offer, such as growth opportunities,
desired flexibility, or other non-monetary factors.

———

Be honest if you are feeling disappointment
Leave open the opportunity to continue discussions;
it's disruptive and costly to lose a star performer.

———

Don't wait until year-end
There is little benefit to storing up your expectations
and letting them out all at once; no leader enjoys
having that conversation.

Stay on their radar

A follow-up email is a good way to share your appreciation for any feedback given, to summarise next steps and updates, and to remain top of mind even when you are not in the room.

Check in for alignment at the end of the conversation

Ensure everyone leaves with the same understanding and agreement on next steps.

"My salary situation at 'Morning Joe' wasn't right. I made five attempts to fix it, then realized I'd made the same mistake every time: I apologized for asking."

MIKA BRZEZINSKI

When offered a new role

*Sometimes when you are offered the role of
your dreams, it can come quite suddenly and
unexpectedly. You have always wanted the role...
someday. But today you feel unprepared, nervous or
even consider declining because you think you will
be better after a few more years of learning in your
current role.*

*Other times you can be asked to take a role you had
never considered. One that is possibly not aligned
with what you had planned to do long term. Before
you get stuck over-thinking this unexpected offer,
clear your head with a few reflective questions.*

What are the potential upsides and downsides?

———

Will you regret your decision in 12 months, or will you be celebrating that you stepped into discomfort?

———

If you welcome the challenge, will you be able to take actions in the future that steer you toward success in a different, but equally satisfying direction?

———

Are there people you trust who are able to see something you can't see in yourself?

———

Are you crystal clear on your career trajectory or is there room for a different experience that would enhance your resume for the next bigger role?

"Do not
wait until
the conditions
are perfect
to begin.
Beginning
makes the
conditions
perfect."

ALAN COHEN

What would the most confident version
of yourself do?

——

Listen to your intuition.

——

Nerves are the same feeling as excitement.
Reflection will help you figure out if the opportunities
is a scary change or a dangerous one.

Moving into a new position

The first 90 days for any new leader is a critical period. It's a time for building relationships, understanding the organizational culture, and establishing credibility. Successful leaders use this time with intention to prioritize learning, communication, and strategic planning to navigate the complexities of their new role and lay a solid foundation for their long-term success.

Make the hard decisions on personnel early
No CEO says, "I wish I had taken longer".

———

Evaluate your bench strength
Do you have the right people in the right seats?

———

Be focused and prioritise
Don't bite off more than you can chew. There is enormous opportunity across the business. Everything looks good on paper and then you have to execute.

———

Learn to say "no" to lower priority items
In the first few months, you will receive tons
of feedback.

———

What do you need to be successful?
What are the 3 decisions you need to make?

———

Go on a listening tour
Be prepared and intentional. What questions do you
want to ask clients, team, and internal stakeholders?

———

Schedule structured meeting times with your team
Get to know them on a personal level.

—

**Have a structured way of scoring the relevance
and impact of opportunities.**
Create an analytical framework by which to measure
opportunities, make decisions and prioritise.

—

Have a clear vision and roadmap in 6 months.
Involve your senior people in its development.

—

Don't stress.
You've got this!

"*Don't let the fear of striking out hold you back.*"

BABE RUTH

Personal brand in action

Your personal brand is the authentic external reflection of who you are in the eyes of those who experience you. The challenge is that sometimes there is a gap between how we see ourselves compared to what others think. It is not easy to close this perception gap, but the best way to start is by asking questions, being open to feedback, and acting on the feedback you receive.

Below are some tips for understanding what your personal brand is and how to manage it toward what you want your personal brand to be.

———

Ensure there is synergy between your brand and your everyday behaviours.

———

There is no replacement for substance. Knowing what you're doing, having integrity, and working at a consistently high level is the best way to succeed.

———

Be self-aware and know how people respond to you. Adapt if you realize, either through observation or feedback, that people are not experiencing you in the way you want.

———

Gather diverse sources of feedback. Seek input from different people so you have multiple points of view.

———

Manage your emotional triggers. When you ask for honest feedback, be prepared to receive some negative comments. Constructive feedback is important for self-growth and development.

———

Understand how narrow or broad your exposure is. Organise skip level meetings outside of your direct chain of command to learn more about different business areas.

———

Be able to describe what you do in 10-15 seconds.
Be prepared and always ready for those moments.

———

Being a constant self-promoter is off putting,
so focus on achievements that have a broad business
impact and support your desired personal brand
and overall reputation.

———

Practice public speaking and communication.
Your voice is one of your biggest assets.

*"Be yourself.
Everyone else is
already taken."*

OSCAR WILDE

Accepting Feedback

Asking for feedback is an excellent way to grow. But asking is not always easy because it can run counter to our need for acceptance. What can feel like personal criticism can easily trigger our antiquated survival mechanism that runs deep and put us into defensive mode.

The best leaders understand the value of getting feedback. It is instrumental in helping them to realise their full potential and also understand their blindspots.

———

Ask for specifics. Feedback is often shared as headlines that are too vague to be helpful.

———

Solicit regular 360-degree feedback to understand where you are most effective and what may be your blindspots.

———

Leave your ego at the door. If you have a heartbeat,
you have blindspots.

———

Be mindful of the polished apple. As a leader you
won't always hear the true story unless you seek it out.

———

Don't be afraid of feedback. It is not eternal
judgement. At the same time, don't take feedback
from somebody you wouldn't take advice from.

———

Create a 'Learn it All' culture not a 'Know it All' one.
Create an environment of open feedback loops where
people can approach you with feedback.

*"Faults are more
easily recognised
in the works
of others than
in our own"*

LEONARDO DA VINCI

———

Listen with the intent to understand. Recognise your triggers so you don't get defensive.

———

The best way to get more feedback is to show appreciation and take action to address it.

———

Get real-time feedback when possible. The most specific and actionable feedback will be when a situation is still fresh in the minds of the giver and receiver.

Self-compassion

To experience a life of happiness, optimism, curiosity, and connection, it is important to be able to extend compassion to yourself as you do to others. This includes being kind to yourself when facing a painful situation, recognizing that failure and suffering is a human experience we all share, and maintaining a balanced approach to negative emotions.

Things will not always go perfectly. Left unchecked, you may focus on negative feelings that trigger an overwhelming feeling of self-pity. Or, self-compassion can help you respond to the disappointment with empathy and unconditional self-acceptance. The process of turning compassion inward is a powerful source of coping with challenges and it may take some practice to give ourselves the same kindness we would give to a friend.

Embrace your emotions
They are part of the human experience.

—

Talk to yourself as you would a good friend
How would a close friend react if they were to hear
your inner dialogue?

—

Remember, it's okay not to be okay
Give yourself permission to feel.

—

See mistakes as lessons, not failures
They shape growth.

—

Breathe through the stress
Know this is a moment, not a lifetime.

—

Prioritize mental peace
Know and understand that self-criticism
doesn't serve you.

——

Celebrate the small wins
More importantly, know how far you've come.

——

Let go of comparisons
Your journey is uniquely yours.

——

Reach out when it gets heavy
Vulnerability is strength.

——

Fuel actions with self-love,
not unkind judgment.

——

Self-compassion isn't a destination
It is a daily practice in understanding and kindness.

"The real difficulty is to overcome how you think about yourself."

MAYA ANGELOU

Career Crossroads

"I was at the highest point in my professional career, whilst feeling the lowest about it."

Many of us have been there. A feeling of burn out that is overwhelming and leaves you feeling frustrated, frazzled and joyless. When you are meeting the company needs but not your own, it is time to listen to the wisdom of your inner voice that is yearning for something more. Even if you are not quite sure yet what that something is, there are some important steps you can take to regain control of your path forward.

Take control of your career
Be the pilot, not the passenger.

**Don't wait for a life event to gain clarity
on your priorities**
You don't need to hit rock bottom to make a change.

———

Create space in your day for self-inquiry
Confirm what matters to you and drives you to
perform with wholehearted enthusiasm.

———

Check-in on your intrinsic motivators
Make a list of what you love most in a role, such
as the types of people you enjoy working with,
the components of a role you find fulfilling, the
environment, culture, and level of autonomy. Set this
list against any role you are considering.

———

Create your personal "Board of Directors"
Find people who will be your truth-tellers and ask the
questions you may not be asking of yourself.

———

Listen to your gut
It will offer valuable intel if you choose to listen.

———

Your energy is a valuable commodity
Find a role which fills you up rather than depletes you.

Make time for reflection
It is important to make the time to define your goals,
create a plan, and be strategic about your career path.

Your energy is infectious
Doing a job you don't enjoy will negatively impact
those around you because they are the ones who
experience you when the corporate mask comes off.

Just because you are good at something doesn't mean it is what you have to do
Stop doing work that makes you want to hit the
snooze button every morning.

Financial discipline creates financial security
There may come a time when you want to take a
career pause in order to return to center. Investing
wisely now can help give you options in the future
that you may not otherwise have.

WITH SPECIAL THANKS TO TRACY RUCKER WILSON
FOR HER CONTRIBUTIONS TO THIS GUIDE

"*Knowing thyself is
the beginning of
all wisdom.*"

ARISTOTLE

Self-Management

Regulate your own behaviors, emotions, and actions

Self-management is a crucial skill for highly effectively leaders.

Leaders who master their emotions and make sound decisions will inspire their team's confidence. Leaders who demonstrate self-control and resilience create a positive work environment that is rooted in trust and respect. Leaders who navigate challenges in a calm and effective manner create a stronger focus on organizational goals. Leaders who exemplify all of these qualities have mastered self-management and are more likely to inspire their team members to cultivate similar qualities. That contributes to a powerful culture of teamwork and productivity within their organization.

Leaders set the tone

A company's well-ingrained culture can be a competitive advantage. Extraordinary leaders understand that a culture is created by its people and everybody in a company plays a vital part in creating and perpetuating the culture and the company values. It's not what is written on the wall, it's what you do every day, and it starts with you.

—

A set of corporate values isn't enough. Those values need to translate into everyday actions and behaviors.

—

What is modeled at the top sets the tone and the standards that permeate throughout an organisation.

—

A high-impact environment is created by leaders delivering consistent signals. Consistency is how you show up and what you do every day.

———

Small actions make a difference. Small actions multiplied help you achieve big things. Leaders who are intentional at building trust on their team one day at a time creates a winning team.

———

Specific behaviours show an individuals' attitude.

———

Hire for culture as well as for capability and competence.

———

Celebrate and reward individuals who personify the the organisational values.

———

Be willing to hire and fire based on the company's core values. Ensure the qualities and behaviours of the individual exemplify the culture and do not undermine it.

A company culture is only as strong as its' worst
tolerated behaviour.

People in healthy organisations admit what
they do not know, identify the issues, and recover
quickly from mistakes.

Create a collective sense of ownership
for the company's top priorities. Their success
is your success.

Words are just words. You can talk about your
cultural values, but it is your behaviours that matter.
This means walking the talk.

"The competitive difference is not in deciding what to do, but in how to do it"

LARRY BOSSIDY

Emotionally intelligent leadership

Just as people have a wide range of intellectual abilities, there are a wide range of emotional skills that impact the way we think and feel inwardly as well as how we act and behave outwardly.

Great leaders are expected to inspire, empower, and engage their team to create exceptional results, but even the best leaders will struggle when emotions get in the way and stifle their rational thinking. Being emotionally intelligent enables a leader to handle complex interpersonal relationships while bringing out the best in others, and this means learning how to make your emotions work for you instead of against you.

Recognize your emotional, relational, and situational triggers.

—

Emotions are reactions that may not be based
on facts.

—

When emotionally triggered, practice empathy by
putting yourself in the other person's shoes.

—

Emotions are contagious.
Remember that a smile can brighten someone's
day as easily as a cross word can ruin it.

—

Infallible composure is not emotional intelligence.

—

All emotions are transitionary. Don't get stuck there.

—

Don't project the present moment into
the foreseeable future.

> ## "Yesterday I was clever, so I wanted to change the world. Today I am wise, so I am changing myself"

ANON

It's ok to have bad days. Everyone does.

———

Learn how to disagree without being disagreeable.

———

Don't burn any bridges. You may have to cross the same river in the future.

———

Never make a permanent decision on a temporary emotion.

———

Never overestimate your power to change others.

———

Never underestimate the power to change yourself.

Creating an inclusive environment

Research shows that diverse companies often produce stronger business results. But if the environment is not an inclusive one, the benefits of a diversified organization will never be realized. Strong employee engagement requires more than occasional recognition with a pay increase. Similarly, inclusive environments require each employee to experience shared positive experiences with emotional connection.

Achieving diversity and inclusion goals may sound like a daunting ambition, but there are some very practical steps a leader can take toward creating a team that is set up for success.

———

Recruit from diverse sources. If your team looks like the top university lacrosse team, chances are you need to expand the reach of your recruiting efforts.

———

You can only attract people who see themselves
represented on the team, so the interviewers
and leadership team need to represent a diverse
spectrum of talent.

———

Create an environment that fosters workplace
flexibility. Leaders who provide desired flexibility
for the diverse needs of a team are often rewarded
with fierce loyalty.

———

Be genuinely empathetic. You can unite minds
over a common goal, but uniting hearts will get you to
a common understanding of each other and a deeper
level of trust.

———

Help your talent grow and develop.
Continually review available opportunities as a way
to retain your top talent.

———

Create a fair and unbiased promotion process.
Without it, talented diverse talent will walk
out the door.

———

Senior leadership needs to be accountable for
advancing diverse talent at every level. Transparency is
needed when qualified candidates have not advanced.

———

Create a safe space for debate. An inclusive culture
is achieved in an environment of respect and trust
where individual biases can be challenged.

———

Build in space to connect as human-to-human.
Empathy is born from caring, and caring comes from
knowing someone.

WITH SPECIAL THANKS TO ANGIE KARNA AND CAROLINE
BUTLER FOR THEIR CONTRIBUTIONS TO THIS GUIDE

"Diversity is being invited to the party; inclusion is being asked to dance."

VERNĀ MYERS

Setting meeting expectations

Set a firm time limit

Shorter is better as it keeps people focused on the most important points. Don't allow a 15 minute update become a one hour meeting.

Review your diary

Remove yourself from meetings that do not require your input, value or approval. As your priorities change, so should your attendance at standing meetings.

Ensure your assistant knows your priorities

They can help manage your calender if they know what is important to you.

———

Schedule preparation time for upcoming meetings
Focus on what is coming up to ensure you have
enough time to prepare for the audience and what
they need to know.

———

Be clear on your role in the meeting
Your role and amount of advance preparation differs
if you are attending to receive an update, provide
input, or make a decision.

———

**Organise your time linked to the
company objectives**
Have a monthly check point to ensure your time
allocation is in alignment and contributing to the
goals. Course correct as necessary.

Managing your meetings

Your energy introduces you before you even speak. Preparing your energy state before joining a meeting will pay dividends.

———

Your attitude determines your altitude in life. Be mindful of the daily mindset and how it shows up in each meeting.

———

Speak slowly. The pace, volume, and intonation of your speech brings with it status and allows others to fully process your message.

———

Saying a person's name is a power move. It keeps them engaged and will get their attention.

———

Make meeting preparedness an expectation.
Require there to be an agenda for all meetings
and request pre-read material so all attendees are
prepared in advance.

———

Be clear on meeting goals. Define the questions that
need to be answered and by whom. This will improve
your meeting efficiency.

———

When the meeting ends, review the action items.
Ensure no one person has been assigned to, or has
volunteered for, a disproportionate amount of the
work. That includes you.

Giving and receiving feedback

At some of the most senior levels there can be a reluctance to provide direct and candid feedback. In many companies the most valuable and actionable feedback is never given. This is a missed opportunity for both the company and the individual.

Many people want to avoid or delay these conversations because they don't want to deal with an uncomfortable outcome, they lack the time, or they do not work in a feedback-orientated culture. In addition, the basic human desire to be liked can get in the way.

Tips for giving high quality feedback:

—

Share real-time feedback. Feedback shared in the moment is more valuable and it enables the feedback receiver to connect to the event.

—

Speak to the specific behaviour and its effect. Don't personalise it and don't add your own interpretation, commentary or judgement.

—

Always substantiate your feedback. Speaking in headlines isn't valuable to the receiver and it leaves a lot open to interpretation.

—

Dialogue, not monologue. Keep your observation direct and to the point. Invite a response as a two-way conversation will feel more comfortable for both parties.

—

Share the good intention behind your feedback. "I'm giving you these comments because..."

"Be brave enough to start a conversation that matters"

MARGARET WHEATLEY

Make it candid, not candy-coated. You may feel more comfortable giving a gentle message, but the message is more likely to get lost if it isn't delivered in a clear and straightforward way.

Check for alignment at the end of the conversation. By asking "what are you taking away?" you can ensure the message has been understood as intended and there is no ambiguity as to next steps.

Tips when receiving feedback:

If you want your team to be comfortable receiving feedback from you, it's important to model this behaviour and ask for feedback yourself.

—

Listen non-defensively. Don't justify yourself, argue or make excuses even if you disagree. Simply thank them for taking the time.

—

You can show you are open to feedback by evidencing that you have adapted feedback received.

—

If you become triggered in the moment when receiving feedback, pause and reflect on it at a later time. When you look beyond your trigger, there will often be valuable insight.

—

API – Assume Positive Intent when hearing feedback from others.

—

Diversify your sources of feedback. Find different people you trust to give you multiple points of view.

Conducting year-end reviews

Does anybody enjoy that time of year when thoughts turn to compensation, and you have a revolving door of people who want to share their extraordinary successes and amazing achievements? This is where expectations and reality can come into conflict. It's not a fun way to face the weeks leading up to year-end reviews, but this is where transparency, communication, and advance level-setting can go a long way.

The following suggestions will help you manage team expectations for a fair and transparent process:

—

Provide an economic update and state of the business to the entire team. This macro-view ensures everyone receives the same information so there are no mixed messages.

———

Great managers ensure there will be no major surprises. If you have been giving feedback consistently throughout the year, nothing should come as a shock.

———

Stay positive, whether the news you have to deliver is positive or not. Be clear and be prepared to back-up your decisions with evidence.

———

Set out a future pathway for each individual. It's easier for someone to get bid away from their current role when they are unaware of their current organization's plans.

———

Give specific and tangible feedback to help bridge potential gaps in self-perception and the organization's assessment. People don't know what they don't know.

———

Never allow a meeting about remuneration to end
with any aspect left open to interpretation.

———

Despite efforts to provide regular feedback , you may
find yourself meeting with someone who is hearing
feedback for the first time. Recognize this and allow
time for them to process and respond.

"Make feedback normal. Not a performance review."

ED BATISTA

Leading challenging conversations

Challenging conversations are not enjoyable. Whether you need to push back on a decision or give bad news, these situations can be uncomfortable. Why? Perhaps we worry about not being liked or we don't want to make the other person feel bad. But they care enough to take time for the discussion, even when their time is in short supply.

Extraordinary leaders work at mastering the art of crucial and challenging conversations. They have a playbook, which is necessary because these conversations cannot be avoided as you become more senior in your organization. Below are some key steps in how to think about engaging in a challenging conversation.

Prepare for the conversation

Difficult conversations should be thoughtfully considered as to what, where, and when they should occur. They are not something to improvise and hope for the best.

Difficult conversations are not easy nor are they comfortable. It serves no one if you avoid the conversation. Embrace the discomfort.

Anticipate the expected and unexpected reactions. This will help ensure you are not caught off guard so you can *act* rather than *react*.

Know your triggers and how to manage them so you can stay on point.

Understand that even with the best preparation, not everything is within your control and that is ok.

Manage the conversation

Be clear on the purpose. Remember your intent and the desire outcome.

"The aim of an argument or discussion should not be victory, but progress."

JOSEPH JOUBERT

—

Stick to the facts without interpretation or
generalization. Less is more.

—

Focus on behaviors. Do not personalize the feedback.

—

Ask open ended questions. This will give you
additional valuable information and time to process
your response.

—

Move from a place of certainty to one of curiosity. Be
aware of where you may be making assumptions or
imposing judgement.

—

Embrace the silence. Insights can be gleaned from
silence as well as from speaking.

———

Paraphrase the other person's words. This allows you to check for understanding and demonstrates that you are listening.

———

Acknowledge the other person's point of view. This doesn't mean you agree with everything, but it will make them feel heard.

———

Check in for alignment and repeat for emphasis if necessary. It is important to know they understand the situation and there is no misalignment between what was said and what they heard.

There's always one

No matter where you go, or what success
you have already achieved in your life, there's
always going to be:

—

The person who thinks they are smarter than you.

—

The person who doubts your competence.

—

The person who doesn't support you.

—

The person who wants you to fail.

—

The person who just doesn't like you.

—

The person who feels threatened by you.

—

The person who tries to hold you back from success.

Unfortunately, each of these people exist and they can present themselves in almost any role you have. You will inevitably find that there will be doubters, naysayers, cynics, or skeptics as you ascend the corporate ladder. It's part of the journey.

Getting overly frustrated is not going to help you, but how you manage the situation is within your control.

—

Continue to focus on the task at hand.
Excel at what you do.

—

Maintain an ecosystem of support to give you an outlet and sounding board.

—

Be confident in yourself, your performance that brought you to where you are.

———

Ignore the naysayers. Remember that not every voice counts. You get to choose which ones to listen to.

———

Leverage the believers, those who champion and support you.

———

Feedback is not eternal judgement. Don't allow other people to tell you who you are, especially if they are being unsupportive.

———

Don't let people block or derail you. They are simply obstacles to navigate.

———

Everyone can have a voice, but not everyone has a vote. Figure out which voices to respect and which are irrelevant.

WITH SPECIAL THANKS TO KAREN WARES FOR HER CONTRIBUTIONS TO THIS GUIDE

"*Don't let someone dim your light simply because it's shining in their eyes.*"

UNKNOWN

Dealing with an abrasive leader

Leaders come in all types of packaging. Some are caring and empathetic. And then there are some who seem to enjoy exerting power over their team and have little regard for ruffled feathers.

When you encounter the abrasive leader, there are a few reminders to help you turn the other cheek and not let it ruin your day.

———

Put aside the person. Respect the position.

———

Don't personalise other peoples' reactions to things. It's not about you.

—

Don't bend yourself to fit into another person's style.
Continue being your authentic self.

—

Toxicity directed toward you does not have to
consume you. You can choose what you take in.

—

Identify one thing you can respect in a leader that
will help you find compassion for them when they are
not at their best.

—

Always remember your value and worth.
Never let someone else's words or behaviour rattle
your confidence.

"Respond intelligently even to unintelligent treatment."

LAO TZU

———

Have a cheerleading squad that reminds you of who you really are when you experience self-doubt. In those moments it is easy to focus on the negative, but your 'Power Posse' will bring you back to center.

———

Share your feelings with a trusted ally or your tribe; they will be a powerful sounding board and help you to gain better perspective.

———

If you believe a leader is unaware of the impact of their behaviour, you may want to share how you feel. It is possible they don't know what they don't know.

Speaking to an audience

Whether you're asked to speak before an audience or give a presentation, it's important to prepare not only what you plan to say, but how you're going to say it.

The tips below are helpful reminders for how to have an effective and productive presentation that will achieve the results you are looking for.

———

That sense of anticipation and focus on what you're about to do is a natural physiological response – there is no need to fight it. You may experience this as butterflies, adrenaline, or a slightly faster beating heart. Everyone feels this excitement before public speaking, even the professionals. It's what helps us to perform better.

———

Embrace being nervous before you present. It means you care and people will be more attentive when they feel you are showing up authentically.

—

Be present and put your devices out of sight.
Research shows the mere presence of mobile devices
prevents deeper, more connected conversations.

—

Dress for the outcome you want to achieve.
Know your environment and wear what will make you
feel most confident.

—

Prepare a positive state of mind before
presenting. You will be seen as more approachable,
interactive and open to new ideas.

—

Take a few deep breaths just before you start.
It doesn't matter if this means your audience waits an
extra moment or two.

———

Have a short and punchy hook. A powerful opening
statement for your presentation sets the tone for what
you will say.

———

Speak with brevity and choose words that carry a
higher impact. It's more powerful for a listener.

———

Let go of perfection. There is no need to be
word perfect or have impeccable diction.
An occasional umm, pause or interaction with
the audience is natural.

———

Get to the point quickly when answering questions
and be ready with more information if asked.

WITH SPECIAL THANKS TO JENNIFER MORGAN AND CORINNE
MITCHELL FOR THEIR CONTRIBUTIONS TO THIS GUIDE

"Remember not only to say the right thing in the right place, but far more difficult still, to leave unsaid the wrong thing at the tempting moment."

BENJAMIN FRANKLIN

Communicating in a crisis

In times of crises, leaders are required to respond and yet they walk a tight rope. You can say too much and use language which easily offends or say too little which is taken as you don't care.

Below are lessons for how best to approach:

Acknowledge the situation.

Recognise and connect with those impacted.

Anticipate a backlash if you wait too long.

———

Show empathy. Don't underestimate the impact to those affected by a situation or decision.

———

When you speak form the heart, you will connect with the heart.

———

Create multiple forums and keep an open and ongoing communication.

———

Don't be silent but don't be too loud. Keeping communication on email will reduce your risk.

———

Be "fully human" and lead from a place of genuine caring. When the corporate voice kicks in too much, the message gets diluted.

———

Understand that getting it perfectly right
isn't a realistic benchmark. Just aim to not get
it terribly wrong.

———

It's ok to admit what you don't know. Invite those
impacted by the crisis to educate you.

———

Keep your words simple, honest and true for
maximum impact.

———

Do not use comparisons or personal examples in
attempt to show you "understand". It's natural to want
to personalize but it could create a false equivalence.

WITH SPECIAL THANKS TO CAROLINE BUTLER FOR HER
CONTRIBUTIONS TO THIS GUIDE

"The secret of crisis management is not good vs bad; it's preventing the bad from getting worse."

ANDY GILMAN

Self-Care

Maintaining your mental, emotional, and physical health

Self-care is recognizing and responding to personal needs, whether they be rest, relaxation, or recreation. Regular self-care is essential for preventing burnout, which is all too prevalent in today's complex world. It can include simply daily rituals such as getting adequate sleep and exercise, eating nutritious meals, and practicing moments of mindfulness. Ultimately, prioritizing self-care not only enhances individual happiness but it contributes to a more balanced and fulfilling life.

Maximizing your downtime

—

Learning to unplug

—

Resilience during the holidays

—

Surviving business travel

—

Energy management

—

Having a do *not* list

—

Have a trusted circle

—

Stress management

—

Returning from parental leave

—

Forget about having it all

—

Find beauty in simplicity

—

Connecting mind, body & spirit

—

Create good sleep habits

—

Laughter is the best medicine

Walk Slowly

By Donna Faulds

It only takes a reminder to breathe,
a moment to be still, and just like that,
something in me settles, softens, makes
space for imperfection. The harsh voice
of judgment drops to a whisper and I
remember again that life isn't a relay
race; that we will all cross the finish
line; that waking up to life is what we
were born for. As many times as I forget,
catch myself charging forward
without even knowing where I'm going,
that many times I can make the choice
to stop, to breathe, and be, and walk
slowly into the mystery

Maximizing your downtime

The world is a busy place and life will make you as overcommitted as you allow. It is easy to find yourself overwhelmed, overextended, and overcommitted. A 6-month sabbatical may sound nice, but simply having an unscheduled afternoon could be enough to help you get through the next sprint until you have time for a proper holiday to fully relax.

Whether you have a few days or only a few hours to take a break, here are some tips that will help maximize the benefits from your downtime.

—

Listen to your body
It often knows what you need before your mind admits it.

—

Silence the noise
Step away, even if it's just for a few quiet moments. Sun and fresh air do wonders.

—

Take a pause

Know that downtime is not a sign of retreat but
wisdom in action so you can leap further.

—

Rest is more than napping on the sofa

Rest is anything that makes our nervous system feel
safe enough.

—

Rediscover hobbies

Sometimes, a pause means diving into passions you
had pushed aside.

—

Let go of perfection

It's okay if you do not have everything in order
all the time.

—

Connect with loved ones

A conversation, a laugh – they work wonders.

—

Take a digital detox
Technology is a tool, not a tether.

—

Breathe deeply
Meditation and mindfulness can recenter the
wandering mind.

—

Prioritize self-care
A day without plans can rejuvenate.

—

Reflect and journal
Be introspective and realign with your goals.

—

Breaks aren't a luxury
Think of planned breaks as a necessity
for long-term success and well-being.

"Instead of asking, 'have I worked hard enough to deserve a rest?' ask 'have I rested enough to do my most meaningful work?'"

NICOLA HOBBS

Learning to Unplug

There is tension with being a leader in today's world. The role requires zeal and energy and yet the demands can lead to exhaustion. There's a phrase in Italian, 'Dolce Far Niente', that translates to the sweetness of doing nothing. Sometimes relaxing in carefree idleness is time perfectly well spent.

These tips are relevant to anyone, at any level, who has a need to unplug from technology and plug into human connections.

Leave a purposefully phrased out of office notification

Are you on business travel or a personal vacation? Do you plan check and respond to emails while you're away? Will you be available for emergencies that arise?

———

Resist providing your direct contact information

Assign a delegate to determine whether they need to contact you or they can handle issues that arise in your absence.

Create your boundaries

If you need to work on holiday, box the time and stick to it. Share your plans with your family, friends or significant other.

Prioritize your actions

Be realistic about what is achievable to complete before, during, and after your holiday.

Maintain a "not-to-do" list when on holiday

Make a commitment to avoid activities that activate your work brain.

Know what rest looks like for you

Give yourself permission to do those activities during the holidays. Sleep longer, exercise less, immerse yourself into a book for hours, listen to a podcast while watching the scenery.

—

Be where your feet are
If your mind is at work, you may as well be in the office. Those around you will feel your absence.

—

Taking a proper holiday is a good business decision
Your mindset and well-being are key to your sustainability in the seat.

—

**Hold yourself accountable to keep
your vacation promises**
Give yourself a holiday challenge, such as doing a push-up for every email you respond to. You'll either have triceps of steel or it will increase your discipline to leave your phone alone.

—

What's the worst that can happen if you slow down?
If you have a team, trust them and trust their leadership will sustain your business area during your short absence.

"*Almost everything will work again if you unplug it for a few minutes... including you.*"

ANNE LAMOTT

Resilience during the holidays

Is it time to be jolly or does the endless list of parties to plan, gifts to send, and people to thank leave you frazzled? When you consider the work that goes into planning a perfect holiday, you can already feel depleted before you have time you say, "let the vacation begin!".

These tips will hopefully help you have a peaceful and enjoyable holiday!

Peace over pace
Review your diary to see where you are over-stretched and where you can create downtime. Holidays are a time to slow down, recharge, and reconnect.

———

Presence over presents
Being truly present is a gift. Being distracted and lacking focus can have a negative impact on those who are with you.

—

Protect your time
Time doesn't give refunds, so be intentional
with where and with whom you spend it.

—

Plan and prioritise your wellbeing
If you want time to do yoga, hang out at the pub, or
see an old friend, schedule it in your diary. Prioritise
your time and fiercely protect it.

—

Pressure off
Relax the expectations you place on yourself. Some
of the best Christmas movies focus on things going
horribly wrong. Embrace the messiness.

—

Pause
It's important to give yourself permission to take a
break and not try to please everyone.

"People will forget what you said, but they will remember how you made them feel".

MAYA ANGELOU

—

Practise what you preach
You tell your friends and colleagues to switch off, and
you should too. Throw yourself into home life with the
level of energy you usually reserve for work. If you're
feeling really bold, put your phone in airplane mode —
even when you're cruising at only three feet!

—

Permission
Allow yourself to let some traditions go. What once
was fun may have outlived its lifecycle.

—

Press pause and park the devices
It will change how you feel for the better!

Surviving business travel

Travel these days can be filled with stress from crowded airports, unexpected delays, missed connections, and lost luggage.

Remember: a journey can be more than a means to an end. It also provides us with many opportunities as long as we are looking out for them. The power of positive thinking goes a long way for successful travel, and below are some recommendations to make your next business trip more tolerable —
if not outright enjoyable.

—

With a passport, phone, and credit card you can conquer the world.

———

We spend our lives wishing we had more time. Here's time in abundance. A long journey is a chance to read, think and create.

———

Don't forget to pack your patience...and your sense of humour (especially when your flight is delayed).

———

Be polite to the staff. It's not their fault when they need to be the bearer of bad news.

———

Bring a book or download a movie. When you have a long delay, that's a great opportunity to catch up on the novel you've been meaning to read.

But positive thinking only goes so far. You need to be prepared for the expected... and the unexpected.

Preparation is key

- Have a travel checklist.
- Make a to-go bag if you travel frequently.
- Check the local weather before pack.
- Allow sufficient time for airport security.
- Avoid the surprise of an expired passport by getting it renewed 6 months in advance.
- The more important the meeting, the longer the buffer needed after your scheduled landing.
- Pre-book your meal if you have any dietary restrictions.

Enjoy the flight

- Fully charge your electronics before leaving, as not all regional jets have outlets.
- Take your own healthy protein-rich snacks.
- Stay well hydrated when flying.
- If sitting next to someone who wants to chat, be polite but set your boundaries.
- Use noise canceling headphones to help block out cabin chatter or unhappy children.
- Don't feel obliged to work. Take time to rest or have a little fun by watching that movie you've been putting off!

Pack like a pro

- Travel with carry-on luggage when possible.
- If you check a bag, put something distinctive on your suitcase so it is easily recognizable.
- Pack a tracker in your checked luggage to help locate anything that goes missing.
- Go through your daily routines to remember medications and any other essentials.
- A spare outfit is always a good idea just in case of the unexpected.
- You will never regret having a pair of comfortable shoes, even for a one-day trip.

Smooth arrival

- Bring a little bit of local currency in case there's an issue with your credit card.
- Pre-booked your ground transportation.
- Consider the public transportation options if you're arriving at rush hour.
- Collect your miles so you qualify for upgrades, lounge access, and other benefits.
- If you have access to a priority lounge, use it to freshen up upon arrival.
- If you've traveled smart, you can bring you're A-game!

"I have found out that there ain't no surer way to find out whether you like the people or hate them than to travel with them."

MARK TWAIN

WITH SPECIAL THANKS TO JULIE ARMSTRONG, CATHERINE CLAY, NICHOLA HUNTER, DAWN MARINACCIO, KAREN WARES, NICOLA WHITE, AND TRACY RUCKER WILSON FOR THEIR CONTRIBUTIONS TO THIS GUIDE

Energy management

Time is a finite resource and everybody in the world has the same 24-hours in a day. But, unlike time, energy becomes a renewable resource when you build in consistent rituals and habits to better manage and restore your energy. It can also restore your physical and mental health.

Your health is your number one commodity. Wouldn't it make sense to be your number one priority?

Remember that it is easier to maintain your health than to reclaim it. If you don't make time now to prioritise your health, you will be making time later for illness.

Your body is always whispering to you. Listen to it. Your wellness takes less time to sustain than it takes to heal from illness, injury and burnout.

———

You are just one human being, and no one person has infinite capacity.

———

Do not confuse your capability with your capacity. Your unscheduled time is not your availability for others.

———

Your energetic bankruptcy serves no one. You being replenished serves everyone.

———

What you are not changing, you are choosing. Bad habits prevent you from operating in a place of balance.

———

Sleep is part of your professional armoury. You may be able to cope on less sleep, but at what cost and for how long?

—

Make time to be outdoors. Movement is medicine that
is good for your mind and body.

—

Slow down and pace yourself. It is possible to deliver
results without sacrificing your well-being.

—

Don't let long breaks get in the way of short breaks.
Breaks throughout the day and week are just as
important for your recovery as a two-week holiday.

—

It's not just about performance and career longevity;
it's also about the enjoyment of life itself. The journey
is everything.

WITH SPECIAL THANKS TO SUZY READING FOR
HER CONTRIBUTIONS TO THIS GUIDE

"*Being still does not mean don't move. It means move in peace.*"

E'YEN A. GARDNER

Having a do *not* list

Do you find yourself working harder, going faster, and adding more items to your ever-growing 'to do' list? In our world of busyness, the last thing we need is more to-do items on our list. What we really need is a not to do list!

——

Do not expect quality connections with those you love when attached to your devices. Set technology-free times to make lasting family connections.

——

Do not go to bed late and expect to wake up feeling refreshed. Sleep quantity (and quality) is important for your health and good spirits.

——

Do not immediately respond to each incoming message. They are not all of equal urgency.

Do not rush to get every task done. Sometimes going slow is the fastest way to success.

Do not become somebody else's concierge. Sometimes people need to figure things out on their own.

Do not be the person who leaves every meeting with the most action items. Learn when to accept, when to deflect, and when to decline.

Do not say yes when you want to say no. Think about your response before responding instinctively.

———

Do not wait until the deadline to start working on
your most important deliverables. Plan ahead, manage
your time, and delegate other tasks if necessary.

———

Do not please everyone else and forget to
please yourself.

*"There is more
to life than
increasing its
speed."*

MOHANDAS K. GANDHI

Have a trusted circle

Modern-day leaders operate under ever-changing expectations and there are few places where they can fully be themselves. Leaders are expected to be perfect in an imperfect world.

Many will confidentially speak to the loneliness of leadership, but there is a discernible difference between feeling alone and being alone. Most leaders are surrounded by friends, family, and teams of people, yet they can still feel isolated.

Human beings are biologically wired for social connections. Nobody is an island, and that includes even the most senior of leaders. We all need a trusted tribe around us.

Keep these in mind when creating your own safe place to talk, discuss, and vent that is free from judgement or consequence.

———

Maintain a trusted inner circle. Having a valuable internal board of directors won't happen by chance. You need to identify and invest in your tribe.

———

Be selective with the members in your trusted outlet. It's a privileged spot. Select people you trust who have your best interests at heart.

———

Be specific with the hats you need each person to wear. It may be the truthteller who won't sugar-coat reality; the sounding board who will listen; the advisor who will offer guidance; your accountability partner.

———

Expect to be asked the tough questions. One way to continuously improve is to be aware of your blindspots and challenged in your thinking. It may not always be comfortable, but it is important for your development.

It's ok to not be ok. People can forget leaders are human who may be dealing with personal stress themselves. You don't have to bury your emotions and pretend they don't exist. We all need a place to vent and an outlet for releasing the pressure valve.

—

We can't bury feelings alive. Others may not see the tension you're carrying, but it will be like an invisible rucksack of heavy boulders that will impact how you show up and how people experience you.

—

Have people in your circle who are fun. Life is serious enough. Spend time with people who bring enjoyment. Your feelings and emotions will be positively impacted.

"I feel homesick yet I am at home."

SARAH SILVERMAN

Stress management

It's interesting, isn't it? Our pet gets sick, we take them to the vet. A child is unwell, we book a doctor appointment. Our car breaks down, we take it to the garage for maintenance. A device is low on battery, we plug it in.

But do you give yourself the same level of care? Where do you feature on your priority list? Hopefully it is not near the bottom as it is for many people. Your body and mind need to last you a lifetime and you must be take care of them.

—

Listen to your body whispers. Your body is always talking to you – whether it's the cold that takes longer to recover from or the chronic back condition — if you don't listen to the whispers, your body will light roadside flares which are not as easy to bounce back from.

———

Make time to be outdoors. It's not just the vitamin D we need. Movement is medicine.

———

Review your priority list. Where do you feature? What would an upgrade look like?

———

Know what habits are restorative or punitive to your health. Our energy is like a bank account – the debits are ok, so long as they are offset by credits.

———

Don't let long breaks get in way of the short breaks. It's important to still take long weekends and breaks during the day. Sports athletes refer to this as QRT: Quality Recovery Time. They know this will allow them to come back faster, fitter, and stronger.

"There cannot be a
stressful crisis next
week. My schedule
is already full."

HENRY KISSINGER

———

What you are not changing, you are choosing. What bad habits are preventing you from operating from a place of balance?

———

Review your energy gauge. Recognise where you are trending towards burnout. Don't wait for pain or illness to stop you in your tracks.

Returning from parental leave

Don't leave until you leave
Your parental leave starts before the baby is born.
What do you want to be remembered for to set
yourself up for success when you return?

———

**Communicate your return plans clearly
and with confidence**
Make your schedule as predictable as possible and
understand that adjustments may be needed along
the way.

———

Returning to work is a process
Resist taking your emotional temperature during your
first few weeks back on the job.

———

Sync your schedule with your energy
In the early days it's more about managing your
energy than managing your time.

———

Run your own race
Only compare yourself to who you were yesterday.
Having a newborn at home can be a rollercoaster.
What will success look like 3 months from now?

———

Consider "Keep in touch days"
Stay in touch every couple of months before going
back to work. In the UK you can use up to 10 days
during your leave to attend important meetings,
conferences, or training.

———

Plan your new routine and have a backup plan
Design your new daily routine and work out
the details – nanny, daycare, feeding plan, and
most importantly a backup plan in case the baby
(or the nanny) gets sick.

—

Consider flexible arrangements
What does the optimal blend of working from home/
office look like for you? Schedule your first day for
later in the week so your first week back at work is a
short one.

—

Have a strong support group
There will be times when you'll want to throw in
the towel. Have someone to talk to who has been
through the same and can assure you it will get
better and easier.

—

The imposter syndrome is normal
Most new mothers experience a crisis of confidence.

—

**Don't make the first day you go back to work the
first day your child goes to a new caregiver**
Do practice runs to get you and your child
accustomed to the situation.

Forget about having it all

Most people want three things: to succeed at work, to be present and loving with their families, and not sacrifice themselves in the process. The challenge is how to simultaneously do those three things without borrowing from one to fund the other.

Setting our own parameters for success allows us to take back control.

"All" is subjective and ever-changing. Identify what truly matters to you at this moment in your life.

The true measure of success is a calm nervous system. What is it like to be in your head?

———

Instead of measuring time, measure your energy.
What people, places and habits fill you with energy?
Small tweaks can lead to big changes.

———

Mastery of life is not a question of control but of
finding a balance between doing and being.
In addition to your 'To-Do' list, what needs to be
on your 'To-Be' list?

———

The belief that we can easily balance high-powered
careers and parenthood is contrasted with the
reality many of us face. It's possible to do both but
there will be tradeoffs.

———

Embrace the beauty of the present and let go
of controlling your tomorrow.

———

Define your own version of success. Set clear boundaries between work and personal time.

———

Accept the inevitable ebbs and flows of life. It's okay to not always be on top.

———

Balance is a journey, not a destination. Continuously reassess and adjust.

———

A successful career doesn't always mean climbing the ladder; it's about fulfillment.

———

Pause to celebrate your achievements. Don't miss a powerful motivational opportunity for yourself and those around you.

"It isn't normal to know what we want. It is a rare and difficult psychological achievement."

ALAIN DE BOTTON

Find beauty in simplicity

It's easy to get lulled into thinking that we need more to be happy, but the reality is most of us have more than we really need. By simplifying the possessions, people and commitments in your life, you open up space to focus more clearly on personal goals and finding authentic happiness.

These recommendations are to help you take a step back and find areas in which to simplify your life.

—

Create a morning ritual. Get your morning off to a positive and productive start the night before by laying out your clothes and getting to bed at a reasonable time.

—

Downsize everything. Enjoy aspects of being a minimalist by reducing everything from your daily commitments to the contents of your closets.

———

Pursue your dreams, but perfect your present. Focus on the process, not only the outcome.

———

Have clarity in what decisions you are making today and why you are making them.

———

Declutter your space to give yourself additional clarity. Leave things that no longer serve you.

———

Create a distraction-free zone for when you want to do focused work.

———

Take a technology holiday. Temporary breaks from TV, social media, and news can help clear your mind by eliminating information overload.

—

Go paperless if you can. Your desk will be more organized, and you will help reduce your impact on the environment.

—

Create email filters to auto detect and eliminate spam from overwhelming your inbox.

—

Remove toxic people from your life. It takes a village but have people in your life who don't create unnecessary drama.

—

It's not about doing everything but doing what matters most with passion and purpose.

"You have succeeded in life when all you really want is only what you really need."

VERNON HOWARD

Connecting mind, body & spirit

It's easy to underestimate the importance of living a life in balance. The mind guides our perceptions and reactions, the body gives us health and strength to pursue life's adventure, and the spirit provides us with purpose, passion, and our inner compass. It is the three together than makes our life as meaningful as possible.

That's not to say that you will achieve perfect balance in every moment of every day but, if you are mindful and aware, you will recognize when you need to rediscover your center.

—

Understand your inner thoughts and beliefs as it shapes both your perception and reality.

—

Your subconscious mind is invisible, but it heavily influences your life and is largely habit-based.

—

Let go of unhealthy habits that become triggered in the face of challenge.

—

Be mindful of body-mind feedback. The way we think and feel sends a message to our brain that controls how we show up. Two minutes of deep breathing or power posing can change the way you feel and the actions you take as a result.

—

Engage in continuous learning. Feed your mind, and you will remain connected, interested, and engaged to perform at your best.

—

Listen to your body. It often knows what is wrong before your mind admits it.

"Your mind, emotions and body are instruments and the way you align and tune them determines how well you play your life."

HARBHAJAN SINGH YOGI

———

Make time for regular exercise. Strengthening the body helps clear the mind.

———

Ground yourself. Have placeholders in the day to connect to who you are, what matters to you the most, and what brings you alive.

———

Let go of what no longer serves you. Replace the people, situations, and influences that drain you with those that energize you.

———

Balance is a journey, not a destination.

Create good sleep habits

Did you know that human beings are the only species that deliberately deprive themselves of sleep for no apparent gain? Sleep deprivation is sometimes touted like a badge of honor representing a strong work ethic and superhuman qualities. The reality is very different. Studies have shown that your IQ can be lowered by up to 15 points after five successive days of sleeping less than you need.

The impact of sleep habits may not always be externally recognizable, but it is critical to mental and physical well-being. The following suggestions are to help create the conditions for good sleep habits.

Know how much sleep is enough for you, typically 7-8 hours a day for adults.

—

Be careful with the decisions your make when you haven't had enough sleep. It can be dangerous to yourself *and* others. Studies show that sleep deficiency affects your driving ability as much as being intoxicated.

—

Create the conditions that allow you to get good quality sleep. Silence your devices or, better yet, leave them in another room. The way you feel when you are awake depends in part on how well you are able to recover when you're sleeping.

—

Eliminate bad habits that can interfere with your sleep habits. You may want to skip the nightcap or reviewing emails right before bedtime. Sleeping helps to repair our brain by washing away toxins and shielding against neurodegenerative threats.

—

If you don't want to prioritize sleep, then prioritize brain rejuvenation (spoiler alert: it's the same thing). Every night's sleep sharpens your memory and decision-making capabilities.

———

Embrace emotional balance. Well-rested nights lead to brighter days and good moods.

———

Try to maintain a fairly consistent sleep schedule every night. Sleeping in on the weekend may be a signal that you're trying to sleep off a debt accumulated during the week.

———

Understand your body's rhythm. It heals and recovers in the silence of the night.

———

Guard your heart. Regular sleep patterns support good cardiovascular health.

———

Unleash creativity. Dive deep into REM sleep to awaken the innovator within.

"Sleep is the Swiss Army knife of health."

MATTHEW WALKER

Laughter is the best medicine

Have you had a bad day that seemed to turnaround as soon as you had a laugh with a good friend? Current research is showing that laughter is not just fun and games. It also has quantifiable physiologic benefits. So, laughter really may be the best medicine and not only is it free, but it carries no adverse side effects! Laughter can be your soul's dance, your heart's melody, and your mind's greatest spark.

———

Recognize laughter's power.
It's medicine without a prescription.

———

Seek joy in the ordinary.
Life's daily quirks offer endless amusement.

———

Embrace mistakes with a chuckle. Perfection is overrated, but a good laugh is priceless.

———

Connect deeply. Shared laughter strengthens
bonds and bridges gaps.

———

Bridge gaps. Humor is humanity's universal language
that helps break barriers and heal souls.

———

Lighten the mood. A joke or witty comment can
defuse tension and uplift spirits.

———

Prioritize mental well-being. Regular laughter reduces
stress hormones and triggers endorphin release.

———

Celebrate resilience. Humor helps us bounce back
much faster than overthinking.

———

Cherish moments of spontaneity.
The best laughs are not planned.

———

Value perspective. Humor provides a fresh lens
to view challenges.

———

Enjoy moments with the youthful enthusiasm
of a child. Laughter is a youthful elixir that keeps
the heart young and spirits high.

"*A day without
laughter is
a day wasted.*"

CHARLIE CHAPLIN

And now it's your turn

Life is chaotic, unpredictable, and uncertain.
Heightened disruption is our new normal and we
don't have to accept it. We can assume our actions
and our choices in isolation won't have an impact,
but they do. Every action creates a ripple of impact.
Our actions compound and there is a multiplier
impact into the world. It's the small actions which
lead to the big shifts.

We are the conscious creator of our life and
experiences. The time is now to take action.
The catalyst for change begins with self. So,
what are you taking agency for? What will you be
celebrating 12 months from now? What impact
will you have had?

It is now time to take your first step towards self
leadership mastery.

Acknowledgements

To Tracy Rucker Wilson, COO of Women In Leadership Global, for your incredible partnership and creativity in bringing this book to life. Your magic is woven throughout every page. You are such an asset to our community and have been a great friend on this journey.

To Anu Aiyengar, Bregje De Best, Martina Cheung, Jane Fraser, Adena Friedman, Isabelle Girolami, Robyn Grew, Mellody Hobson, Jenny Just, Lynn Martin, Sally Moore, Michelle Neal, Jennifer Piepszak, Emily Portney and Dr. Kay Swinburne – all trailblazing female leaders in the industry who are paving the way.

To all the male leaders who have made it their shared commitment to change the face of leadership, including Oliver Albers, Mark Beeston, Doug Cifu, Mazy Dar, Henry Fernandez, Carlos Hernandez, Dave Howson, Adam Kansler, Brad Levy, Rick McVey, Lee Olesky, Yann Robard, David Rutter, Edouard Tavernier, Brad Tully, Lance Uggla and Chris Willcox. Your unwavering investment in female leaders is a testament to your commitment as industry allies.

And to Mark Beeston, Chris Concannon, and Tom Pluta who also serve on our Advisory Board to further elevate the Women In Leadership Global mission.

How to become a WILG member

WILG is tribe which pulls together inspiring and accomplished women from across the financial services sector. These women share a strong commitment to tap into there personal powers and are looking for a powerful peer network.

From Women In Leadership

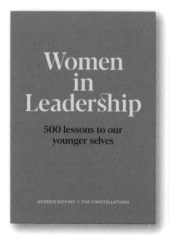

Georgie Dickins is an internationally recognized authority on leadership, sought after speaker, author, and coach. Georgie serves as a trusted advisor to CEOs and changemakers within the financial services industry and appreciated as a modern-day leadership expert by both corporations and the industry titans that lead them alike.

Georgie's 20 years of experience in the financial services industry has given her extensive exposure enabling her to truly understand the requirements of leadership as well as the expectations placed on business leaders.

As the co-founder and managing director of Cajetan, a boutique firm specializing in transformational leadership, Georgie orchestrates impactful change within organizations. She is also the founder behind Women In Leadership Global, a peer network with a mission to advance the face of leadership across the world's most influential industries.

Based in Suffolk, Georgie splits her time between her home, London and New York.

Klaudia Gorczyca is an experienced manager, entrepreneur and an executive performance coach. She spent several years in financial services, moving from trading, to hedge funds, to disruptive tech, and involving management of global teams. She was named as one of 'Women in FinTech Powerlist' by the UK's Innovate Finance.

As the President of Women in Leadership Global, Klaudia is the blueprint and the fuel to people who have been identified as future leaders within their organisations. She helps equip them with skills, behaviors and mindsets required to get to the next level.

Her core passion is cognitive diversity and its role as a catalyst for innovation. As founder of Dialogue Age, Klaudia is committed to driving measurable change by empowering leaders to build high performance, diverse teams, deliver an outstanding performance and magnify their impact.